PREACHING PILGRIMS

Michael E. Williams

An ecumenical guide
to excellence in preaching

DISCIPLESHIP RESOURCES
MATERIALS FOR GROWTH IN CHRISTIAN FAITH AND LIFE
P.O. Box 189 • Nashville, TN 37202 • Phone (615) 340-7285

Also by Michael E. Williams:

Preaching Peers (order no. W132K)

Storytelling: A Journey into New Worlds videotape
(order no. PR008VC)

Preaching Christian Stewardship: Leader's Guide, a
study guide for the videotape, *Preaching Christian Stewardship* (order no. ST058L)

Diagrams in chapter 1 © 1987 Kinuko Y. Craft. Used by permission.

Library of Congress Catalog Card No. 88-50640

ISBN 0-88177-062-0

DR062B

CONTENTS

1. Masters   1

2. Life-Worlds   13

3. Jugglers   23

4. Pilgrims   33

5. Peers   56

6. Progress   69

FOREWORD

Many pilgrims have accompanied me on the journey that led to this book. Ray Sells of the Center for Congregational Life first suggested a resource of this type. My colleagues in the Section on Worship—Andy Langford, Hoyt Hickman, and Diana Sanchez—offered encouragement and helpful responses along the way. Three pastors preaching weekly in local congregations read the manuscript: Diane Luton Blum, Robert H. Lewis, and J. William Menees. Among these special thanks go to Diane for pointing me in the direction of Neill Hamilton's work. My discussions with Susan Ruah, especially those related to the language of mastery and maturity, helped to make the language of that portion of the manuscript more precise. Without the assistance of the staff of Discipleship Resources, especially Paul Franklyn and J. Lee Bonnet, you would not be reading this volume. For the friendship of all these colleagues I am grateful. The book is better for their assistance, though its weaknesses must not be placed at their doorstep. Both those of which I am aware and the ones that I will only come to discover after it is printed are my responsibility.

A very special word of gratitude must go to my constant companion on the way, Margaret Perry Williams, who tolerates me when I am intolerable, loves me even when I am unlovable, and appreciates me even when I don't appreciate myself. In more ways than I can say or am even aware she contributes to my life, and thus to this work.

Michael E. Williams
Maundy Thursday, 1988

Chapter 1
MASTERS

J— awakes to the sound of Top Forty radio. Monday again. The sermon preached just yesterday morning seems ages ago. Next Sunday looms on the horizon. Once again to rise and speak a word of comfort, of challenge, and, finally, of God. It never becomes easy, never the simple collection of tasks the preaching course in seminary outlined. Mrs. K— is scheduled for surgery tomorrow in a hospital fifty miles away. There goes Tuesday. Two Bible studies on Wednesday, yet to be prepared. Thursday night Finance and Trustees will have to make urgent decisions about the building. Friday night, wedding rehearsal. Saturday morning, youth bake sale. Saturday afternoon, wedding and reception. Then Sunday again. There is never enough time.

J— turns back the covers and sits on the side of the bed, listening to the weather and traffic reports. Monday again. There will never be enough time. But what if this week there is nothing to say, as well?

B— had been planning for this holy season for months. The lessons had been read and studied, given to the musician, the lay reader, and the altar guild months before. And it was finally here. The sermons were not together just yet, but images had been flowing for weeks, gathered on napkins and notepads and stuffed into file folders. One week would center around the story from scripture for that Sunday, another around a memory from childhood, and a third around a folktale from the church of the Middle Ages. It was exciting to see the pattern of each sermon come together. Sometimes it happened that those insights and patterns emerged in the study, but more often they came in the shower, on the long drive to the hospital, in conversations with newcomers to the church or with members of long standing. Jotted down on anything that was handy or simply repeated until etched into memory, the insights were saved. There were hardly enough hours in the day to take it all in.

It was Monday and, sitting in a favorite chair, the anticipation and adventure of opening this week's file folder was almost too great to bear. Once opened, something of significance would be set loose upon the world. So be it.

"Try hard to show yourself worthy of God's approval, as a laborer who needs not to be ashamed; be straightforward in your proclamation of the truth" (2 Timothy 2:15, NEB).

1

Do you remember that professor in seminary who tried to teach you the one best way to prepare a sermon? Or perhaps it was the book on preaching, which came highly recommended by friends and which outlined the author's basic approach to sermon preparation? Did you go along and work with this one method whether it seemed right for you and your congregation? Or have you rejected your mentors' procedures for your own self-devised plan of action, all the while feeling a little guilty. Perhaps you have given up all attempts to prepare to preach "the way you are supposed to" and have patchèd together a way to get through the week and stand up on Sunday with something (at least) to say? You may even be one of those fortunate preachers who chooses an approach to preaching that suits you and your congregation, feels good about that choice, and is willing to adapt it whenever your needs or the congregation's needs change.

Assumption: We all can grow toward excellence in preaching. Assumption: We do not necessarily grow toward excellence in preaching the same way. Both of these understandings are set upon a single foundation: there is not one way to preach well. In other words, excellence in preaching is available to all of us, but each of us needs to discover the approach to preaching that suits us as preachers, our preaching tradition, and the particular community in which we preach.

Often the pastor in today's church is by necessity a generalist, a "Jack (or Jill) of all trades and master of none." The pastor is asked to be counselor, administrator, teacher, janitor, maintenance person—Oh! and yes, if there is time, to prepare to lead worship and preach. We find ourselves scurrying from one appointment to another meeting, rushing from a luncheon devotional to teach a class, often wondering if this is really what we were called and ordained to do. Most ordination services mention at least two areas of responsibility that the ordained person is set apart to do: word and sacrament.

Both of these have to do with worship, and often become the last two notes on our "to do" list each week. No one will make an appointment to ask if we have taken adequate time to prepare for the sermon, nor will a meeting convene to inquire into our preparation in prayer, silence, and reading aloud to lead the Sunday service. Yet worship is the most public act in which we speak of our faith in the community of faith, in which we share the sacraments that are those "outward and visible signs of an inward and spiritual grace" that move us beyond words into the very presence of the holy.

This is not the situation intended when we sought to follow our inner nudgings toward ordained ministry. Still, this is the situation in which too many of us find ourselves. It may not be possible (or even desirable) to silence the many demands made upon the church from those inside and outside its walls. Notice that the demands are made of the church, the whole Body of Christ composed of all Christians, not clergy alone. There are means of sharing the ministry of many needs with the whole community of faith. But it is not our purpose to outline those here.

Rather, let me suggest that it may be possible for the pastor to become a "Jill (or Jack) of all trades and master of *one*," especially if that one trade is preaching in the context of worship. All the many trades calling for a pastor's time can inform the preparation and delivery of sermons. Weddings, funerals, counseling, hospital visits, even meetings can inform the act of preaching. But only if they are incorporated in the ongoing discipline of study, prayer, and silence that takes place in the time we set aside to listen before we speak.

Excellence, Maturity, Mastery

Geoffrey Chaucer in his *Canterbury Tales* narrates the journey of a group of pilgrims on their way to Canterbury and the tomb of Thomas à Becket. To pass the time along the way the pilgrims decide to tell stories to each other. Soon the reader is so caught up in each traveler's tale that one begins to hope they never reach their destination, that the stories will go on endlessly. It is not the shrine at the end of the journey that captures our imagination but the characters and stories along the way.

Excellence in preaching, like maturity in faith or mastery of a subject or skill, is not a state we reach but a journey we take. Like pilgrims on the way to a shrine, we commit ourselves to the journey, thinking we know the reason for our travel and its value for us when we arrive at our destination. Sometimes, if we keep our eyes and ears open and our wits about us, our imagination is captured by conversations with other pilgrims, or sights along the way, or chance encounters with strangers, or people and places other than the shrine we intended to visit. Often it will be these "incidentals" that make the greatest contribution to our journey.

So, as with Chaucer's pilgrims headed for Canterbury, it is not the end of the journey that makes the going worthwhile. It is the people and stories along the way that give the pilgrimage its value. Each pilgrim will have an essentially different experience of the journey. Each will make a unique contribution to the collective story and undergo unexpected transformations along the way.

Excellence is not a goal, any more than maturity or mastery is an end in itself. Each is a process led forward by an image of what excellence, or maturity, or mastery might be. Yet each is open to novelty and surprise, because the itinerary for the journey is not set in stone, nor is the pilgrim in control of the pilgrimage. The journey toward excellence does not end at some shrine or other but continues as long as the pilgrim lives.

Thus, we will not attempt to describe an ideal state of preparation and delivery of sermons toward which the preacher might strive. Rather we will concern ourselves with the journey and the disciplines that lead to ever greater excellence. These bear many similarities to the two other processes, maturity and mastery.

While we might hope that maturity in faith and the mastery of preaching would go hand in hand, they are not necessarily the same. In recent years those who view human life as a developmental process have written extensively, proposing the various stages or seasons through which we, as humans, pass. The most prolific and highly respected of the developmentalists dealing with issues of faith is James Fowler.

In a recent book, *Becoming Adult, Becoming Christian,* Fowler uses the imagery of journey to describe the process of coming to maturity in faith. In fact, as he compares and contrasts the approaches that he and other developmental theorists take in describing this journey toward maturity, he assesses them according to the image of the good man/good woman which they see as the image of the mature human being.

Fowler outlines the stages of faith development emerging from interviews conducted by him and his associates. These are described fully elsewhere. We name them and give the time of life with which they are usually associated.

Primal Faith: birth to approximately 2 years
Intuitive-Projective Faith: 2 years to approximately 6 or 7 years
Mythic-Literal Faith: 6 or 7 to early adolescence
Synthetic-Conventional Faith: early adolesence to adulthood
Individuative-Reflective Faith: adulthood
Conjunctive Faith: adulthood
Universalizing Faith: adulthood

It is important to note that beyond the first four stages no stage is linked with a specific age. The last three are simply stages of adulthood. It is possible, even likely, to find adults at any of these stages, even very early ones, except for the final stage. Few persons ever come to a universalizing faith stance according to Fowler. It would seem at first glance that the goal of a life aimed at maturity would be this universalizing faith, or at least conjunctive faith. Some of Fowler's sympathetic critics argue for this approach.

Fowler, however, comes to another understanding of the goal of maturity. He assesses the goal of his developmental scheme in these words, "The crucial point to be grasped is that the image of human completion or wholeness offered by faith development theory is not an estate to be obtained or a stage to be realized. Rather, it is a way of being and moving, a way of being on pilgrimage."[1]

An alternative view of maturity to Fowler's is offered by Neill Hamilton in *Maturing in the Christian Life: A Pastor's Guide*. While Fowler begins with the experience of the individual and from that charts a journey toward maturity based upon that testimony, Hamilton begins with the witness of the New Testament and from those testimonies outlines his scheme of Christian maturity.

Beginning at these two different places, it is little wonder that these two theorists come to very different images of the road to maturity. Hamilton takes Fowler to task for presenting a generalized outline of maturity that does not reflect specifically coming to maturity in any one faith. Rather, Hamilton suggests that there is a specifically Christian journey toward maturity in faith, and he attempts to map the road of that journey.

According to Hamilton, there are three phases of the Christian life, each one associated with a character or set of characters in the biblical witness. The three stages are:

1. Faith of the crowd
2. Faith of the disciples
3. Life in the Spirit

The faith of the crowd is characterized by an interest in the exciting and miraculous aspects of the life of faith. Just as the crowds followed Jesus to see what would happen next, so many in the faith are attracted by those elements that are attention-getting. Just as the crowds left Jesus or turned hostile when his ministry moved beyond entertainment, it is easy for those in the crowd stage of faith to lose interest or become disappointed when the entertainment ends.

The faith of the disciples is based upon following the Jesus of history as the example for the life of discipleship. Persons at this phase see their own effort as crucial to building the foundations of God's reign. They believe that the world can be changed for the better and that it is up to them to do just that. The difficulty with this stage, according to Hamilton, is that it relies so heavily on human effort and focuses strongly on the results of human action. It is difficult for those in this leg of the journey when results are not forthcoming.

Life in the Spirit focuses neither on the entertaining aspects of the faith nor on human effort and results. Rather, life in the Spirit centers on the gifts and graces of each person for ministry and the call to community in which these gifts and graces might be exercised. *Calling,* not career, is the word best describing ministry in this phase. Their calling lures persons into the future, into community, and is not dependent for its value on results.

The specific value of Hamilton's view of Christian maturity is that it reflects a peculiarly Christian point of view, and he applies it directly to the role of the pastor in that process. The image of the pastor that Hamilton suggests is that of *"prophetic guide to maturing in the Christian life."*[2] The pastor is a pilgrim who assists others to tell their stories and offer their gifts so that all on the journey move toward maturity.

It is the journey, not the journey's end, that characterizes the road to maturity. Just so, it is the way of excellence rather than some state of achievement that we are seeking to portray. Excellence, like maturity, is a means of learning and growth that is continual and lifelong. Yet excellence is not simply the same as maturity. While we would hope that the preacher is on the way toward maturity, the two are different, for there are numerous skills and abilities involved in preaching that are outside the realm of maturity of faith. We might speak of excellence in preaching in terms of mastery, as well.

Often when we hear the word *mastery* we think of Bach or Rembrandt, Pavlova or Jane Austen—someone in the arts who has mastered the skills of a craft. Or perhaps a basketball or chess player comes to mind, someone who has become master of a game. But can we honestly say that we are seeking mastery in preaching? Does the term *mastery* really apply?

I hesitate to invoke the term *mastery* because it has such disastrous associations for persons who have experienced oppression from a variety of so-called "Masters." Mastery, as it is used here, has nothing to do with the enslavement of one person or group by another. Rather I intend it to refer to the process by which a person, through the practice of certain disciplines, gains an expertise in a specific skill or craft. We speak of a master potter or painter or even a master mechanic. Mastery is not a state to be attained but a quality of the journey of life and faith.

We can, indeed must, seek mastery in our preaching, if we are true to our calling. A story is told of an Asian artist who sat and repeated the same brush stroke time after time after time. An observer asked why he spent so much time and effort on that one stroke rather than simply painting a scene. The artist replied, "One day as I do paint a scene I will need this stroke. By then it will be second nature." The artist was speaking of the discipline and diligence required of anyone seeking mastery.

Paradoxically, through constant discipline we are, in a real sense, the ones who are mastered by our craft. A second nature is added to the first. This second nature is that which has been practiced with fidelity until it seems natural and unpracticed. Just as the dancer's moves seem effortless because of all the effort in rehearsal and at the barre, so the disciplines that allow us to be mastered by our craft bequeath to our preaching the naturalness, the apparent effortlessness, of this second nature.

George Leonard writes of mastery that too often we "assume it requires a special ticket available only to those born with exceptional abilities."[3] He suggests that the realm of persons to whom mastery is available is much larger. "It is available to anyone who is willing to get on the path and stay on it—regardless of age, sex, or experience."[4] Leonard speaks of mastery in terms similar to those we used to describe maturity. He contends, as our definition suggested, that mastery is "not really a goal or a destination but rather a process, a journey."[5]

The process that Leonard outlines does not depend on an "every day in every way I'm getting better and better" mentality. In fact, his description of the "Mastery Curve" is strikingly different from an upward and onward scale of uninterrupted improvement. Leonard envisions the road of mastery in this fashion:[6]

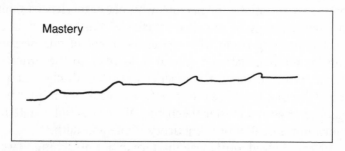

Mastery

The journey of mastery does include periods of clear and decided increases of skill and ability. Yet between those quantum leaps of learning there are long plateaus during which there is no observable improvement. The plateaus can be times of frustration and depression for the one seeking to master a given art or sport.

It seems as if we are stuck, moving neither forward nor backward, and that our effort is in vain.

The plateaus are the most important periods of learning for one on the journey of mastery, because decisions made and actions taken during the plateaus will distinguish the one on the master's way from others. Leonard names three other types according to their responses to the plateaus. They are: the Dabbler, the Obsessive, and the Hacker.[7] All three begin as if on the way to mastery, then something happens.

The Dabbler is an enthusiastic beginner, fascinated by newly found skills and basking in the attention of family, friends, and strangers as the first spurt of improvement progresses. Then comes the plateau. This time of little or no improvement is discouraging and confusing to the Dabbler. Soon the Dabbler decides that this approach is just not working, is just not suited to his or her personality and gives it up in favor of some new approach. Of course, the process is repeated with the new approach which is cast aside as soon as the first plateau comes along.

It is easy to recognize the Dabbler among preachers. The Dabbler picks up on every fad that comes down the pike. This month is a series of dialogue sermons, next month sermons in rhyme, then story sermons told in the person of biblical characters. You can tell which seminar the Dabbler has attended most recently or which book or tape is the current favorite by the form the sermons take that month. Dabbling can wear everyone, including the preacher, out.

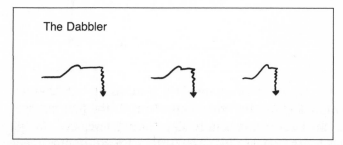

The Dabbler

The Obsessive plunges into any new activity with everything he or she has. Determined to be the best, the Obsessive buys every book and tape available on the favored approach. The initial period of improvement comes as no surprise to the Obsessive, but the first plateau is devastating. Expecting each week to be better than the last, the Obsessive is crushed the very first time the favored approach fails to meet up with the high expectations of unlimited progress. The response is simply to try harder, to work longer hours, to read more books and listen to more tapes. Some weeks will show improvement, only to be followed by weeks of strong setbacks. The task becomes a tiresome and frustrating process and generally ends in a deep sense of personal failure.

The Obsessive among preachers is the one who knows how it ought to be done and then sets out to do it, with a vengeance. Under the pressure of ever having to top last week's effort, this preacher will spend days working to get the sermon letter perfect. Hours will be consumed devising the perfect transition or the most effective turn of phrase. Often when members of a congregation do not appreciate such literary skill, the Obsessive dismisses them as beneath the considerable time and effort spent on preaching. Even so, the Obsessive is rarely satisfied with his or her own work, since it does not progress in the expected steady line of splendor. Whenever a plateau is reached, the Obsessive seeks to overcome by sheer effort what takes time and steady discipline to cultivate.

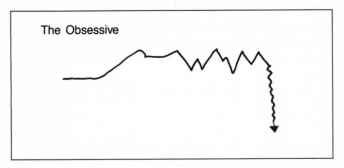

The Obsessive

The Hacker does not mind the plateaus. In fact, after learning the ropes and making some improvement, the first plateau is the place the Hacker moves in to stay. Having developed enough skill to get by, the Hacker looks no further toward improvement. The goal is not excellence but ease. If there is an easy way, the Hacker will take it. If there is a shortcut, the Hacker will know about it, and use it.

The preacher/Hacker buys books of ready-made sermons, sermon outlines, and sermon illustrations and uses them straight— digesting as little as possible on the way through. Often the Hacker has prepared three years of sermons following seminary graduation and just recycles them in church after church. When all else fails, a sermon pilfered from a famous preacher will do just fine. There is little danger that the Hacker will burn out; in fact, there is also little hope of either heat or light being produced in the process.

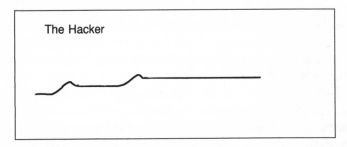

The Hacker

The caricatures of the Dabbler, the Obsessive, and the Hacker above are drawn with bold strokes. They represent the extremes of these characters. Most often among preachers they are seen in other guises. The Dabbler often appears to be imaginative, creative, and up on the "latest thing." The Obsessive is viewed as a hard worker, a scholar, a dedicated craftsperson. The Hacker comes off as easygoing, laid back, and amiable.

Yet, none of these is on the road to mastery. The Dabbler loves the thrill of the new, but will not stick with any one approach with sufficient discipline to move toward excellence. The Obsessive is definitely looking for excellence, even perfection, but is unable to tolerate the long periods of time when little progress is evident. The Hacker is satisfied to be just good enough that it takes little effort to stay at that level and has little interest in improvement.

Leonard suggests that the road to mastery begins as one submits to a disciplined life. Such discipline is not dependent upon constant improvement and exhibits patience on the plateaus of life. A person on the road to mastery is open to new learnings but, unlike the Dabbler, does not fall victim to every fad that comes along. One on the way toward mastery is dedicated to a specific form of discipline but, unlike the Obsessive, is not compelled to make improvement by force. The pilgrim moving toward mastery holds to the chosen discipline faithfully and with patience on each plateau but, unlike the Hacker, is not content to live on any plane forever.

The essence of mastery is surrender. At first this seems paradoxical, but its truth quickly becomes evident. For the preacher it is surrendering to the ongoing discipline of preaching, becoming a "servant of the Word" as H. H. Farmer phrased it almost fifty years ago.[8] Submission, not to some external authority but to an internal and ongoing life of discipline, is a first 'step along the road to mastery. In preaching, as in life, we may follow the guideline Jesus gave to his disciples; those who seek mastery must strive to be servants (Matt. 20:26).

Just as there are many ways to serve, there are also many roads to mastery. This book explores some of them. But more important, it is designed to assist you in discovering your own road to mastery and to keep faith with those disciplines that allow you to become servants of the Word and pilgrims along the road toward excellence in preaching.

1. James W. Fowler, *Becoming Adult, Becoming Human: Adult Development and Christian Faith* (San Francisco: Harper & Row, 1984), p. 74.
2. Neill Q. Hamilton, *Maturing in the Christian Life: A Pastor's Guide* (Philadelphia: Geneva Press, 1984), p. 26.
3. George Leonard, "Playing for Keeps: The Art of Mastery in Sport and Life," *Esquire,* May 1987, p. 113.
4. Ibid.
5. Ibid.
6. Ibid, p. 114.
7. The following discussion is based upon Leonard's description of these three characters, pp. 115-116.
8. H. H. Farmer, *The Servant of the Word* (New York: Charles Scribner's Sons, 1942).

Chapter 2
LIFE-WORLDS

Chaucer's pilgrims run the gamut of ages and life experiences. There is the clerk, the miller, the nun's priest, the wife of Bath, and others. Each has a story to tell and each has a unique perspective from which to tell it. They are all heading for the same destination but have come from many directions and have taken many roads to come to this stage of the journey. They are of different ages, genders, and dispositions. Yet each teller creates a world in the imagination of the others by means of words.

Much the same could be said for any group of pastors who come together on life's road. Any journey begins with a first step and each pilgrim starts from a different place. Each of us has a separate place of birth and family of origin. Each person has a unique series of life experiences and a special story to tell. Yet we as humans share enough in common that we can each hear the stories of the experiences of others with benefit and delight. By means of words we seek to create worlds in the imaginations of our hearers which disclose something of who we are and what we value.

What experiences have contributed to the life-world out of which you preach? What images of family, community, and church inform your view of the persons who listen to your sermons? In what ways have you experienced the world of the scriptures through reading, study, or travel? Where do you begin when you preach? And what path will you take in shaping the sermon?

Is your starting point a given passage of scripture, as with those pastors we have called expository or exegetical preachers? Or do you rather begin by responding to the very specific needs expressed in your congregation or community, an approach Harry Emerson Fosdick championed? Perhaps you organize your sermons around a series of topics which emerge as important for you from your own reading, study, and personal encounters.

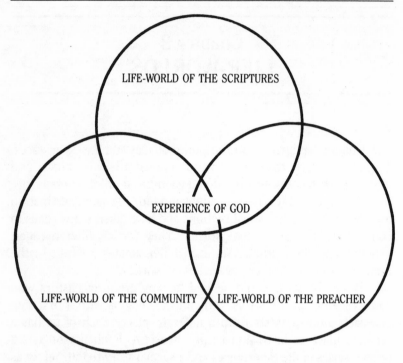

Each of the approaches described above is a significant start-ing place for the journey toward excellence in preaching. Each emerges from an encounter with a particular realm or world. Preaching may begin in the world of the scripture, the life-world of the community, or the life-world of the preacher. While we may begin in any of the three, as with all journeys, we dare not remain in that world alone. Whole preaching must include all three worlds.

The Three Worlds of Preaching

The event of preaching may be described as a coming together of three worlds: the world of the scripture, the life-world of the preacher, and the life-world of the hearers. Each world is com-posed of persons, things, and happenings which shape the context in which our world encounters the other two worlds. Each world overlaps with its companion worlds individually, and at the center of the event of preaching the three worlds converge. This central focus of the preaching event is that encounter with God by means of which lives are transformed. (See diagram.) The LIFE-WORLD OF THE SCRIPTURE is made up of those many worlds from which emerge the stories, poems, legal statements, prophetic utterances, and letters of the Bible. Gerhard von Rad speaks of the importance of this world when he writes, "The task to which we have to do justice has been known and recognized for a long time: we must reproduce the utterance of the Bible in our language just as concretely (just as concretely *ad hominem*) as it was meant in the Bible."[1]

The concreteness of the biblical world keeps our preaching from dissolving into vague theological or spiritual generalities. It keeps us in direct touch with the heritage of our faith and those persons who are a part of the family of faith. The Bible is not a book of philosophical propositions but a book of persons, places, and things. In approaching the scriptures as a source for preaching we enter a world far different from our own. It is this foreign quality, this otherness of the worlds we encounter in the biblical witness, that grasps our imagination and allows us to hear a fresh word from ancient writings.

The worlds of scripture are not fully expressed by a listing of ancient ideas: archaic expressions or outmoded science or philosophy. Nor are the biblical worlds exhausted by the re-creation of living and working spaces and the customs and practices that took place in them. Nor are these worlds limited to the common human experiences and feelings that find expression in the language of the scripture.

In truth the worlds we seek to enter, and into which we hope to lead our hearers, are all of these and more. They are, at the very same time, philosophical and practical, abstract and concrete, strange and familiar, filled with thought and feeling. The tools we bring along to mine the past are our senses, our emotions, and our intellects. Imagination is the medium through which we experience these ancient worlds in as full a manner as humanly possible.

The preacher is called upon to journey into a world of a specific text each week as preparations are made for the sermon. One week we may find ourselves on a hillside in Midian keeping sheep with Moses, and the next week we are on the road between

Moab and Bethlehem with Naomi and Ruth. Even on the same Sunday one reading may leave us in the middle of ancient Corinth, while the next transports us to the shore of the Sea of Galilee. Sometimes a longer narrative or a sequence of stories will allow us to remain in a particular biblical life-world for several weeks in a row.

The entire cycle of the Christian year takes us on an annual journey through the world of an ancient story, the outline of the Gospel narrative. Pastors, by their own choice or by use of such tools as the common lectionary, put flesh on the Christian year's skeletal framework by reading a particular Gospel writer's retelling of the good news for a specific community.

The purpose of the preacher's struggle to enter the world of the scripture is to assist the congregation to enter that world as well. It is in these biblical life-worlds that we encounter and come to know the forebears of our faith and glimpse their faltering attempts to be faithful. In their stories we begin to learn how we might encounter and know the One who is God of the ages, who is still active in our lives today.

The LIFE-WORLD OF THE COMMUNITY is much larger than the congregation of persons to whom sermons are spoken, though they are certainly included. The world of the community includes the population of the neighborhood, town, suburb, or rural area within which the worshiping community gathers. To a great extent the community expands to include the region and nation from which that local group takes many values and toward which a certain loyalty is felt. As the media, especially television, have brought events from the other side of the globe into our living rooms at the moment of their happening, these events begin to shape the consciousness of the world and of the preacher's community, as well.

We can say that there are numerous "worlds" of the community just as there are many and various worlds of the scripture. Preachers need to become familiar with these worlds if they would have their preaching heard. In other words the preacher must learn to speak the language of the congregation and the surrounding communities that shape its way of life.

Learning the language of the congregation is considerably

more than talking with farmers about fertilizer or suburbanites about jogging. James Hopewell writes that every congregation has an idiom by means of which its members communicate. He observes, "What struck me first and most forcefully in these three churches—the one I led and the other two I studied—was the surprisingly rich idiom unique to each. As slight and predictable as the language of a congregation might seem on casual inspection, it actually reflects a complex process of human imagination."[2]

Hopewell suggests that people looking for a church seek "a congregation that catches the intonation of their own language."[3] The pastor must keep ears atuned to pick up the intonations of a particular congregation. The idiom is communicated not simply through choice of words, but through arrangement of space (worship space as well as fellowship space), understanding of time (must the service end at a specific time or does worship continue until everything is finished no matter the length of time), as well as the language used to name their individual and communal experiences (sacred and secular).

The history of a particular congregation and its subgroups (church school classes, for example) will shape the current idiom of these groups. It is wise for the preacher to know these histories and the patron saints (and sinners) of a particular congregation or class, if that pastor would understand its idiom.

The self-perception of the congregation's place in the local community, and its primary influences from other realms (region, nation, and world), are important sources for the preacher to watch and hear. Where do the members of that congregation get their news (newspapers, television, radio); who are the major interpreters of that news who hold authority with them (certain reporters, columnists, or religious broadcasters); what are their sources of entertainment (reading, movies, television, radio); and what kinds of entertainment do they prefer (classical, rock, country, music—sports, public television, or situation comedies on television)?

To preach effectively, the preacher must enter the worlds of the congregation and learn the idiom of those worlds.

The LIFE-WORLD OF THE PREACHER is the third and final

element of preaching that we will consider. Though always present consciously or unconsciously, this is the aspect of the preaching event most often ignored. Many of us were taught to make no personal references. If, however, we could not restrain ourselves, we were to use as few as possible and then speak of our experiences as if they happened to someone else.

It is understandable that these warnings were given. The teachers who suggested them only wished to avoid the abusive and egotistical use of personal stories which cast the preacher as the hero or subject of every story. Yet, too frequently, this attempt to avoid the abuse of the preacher's life story led to sermons that were abstract, a word that had been disembodied. Often they were spoken with an attitude that implied some objective standpoint from which the preacher spoke standing above the ambiguities of daily life. Such an objective standpoint is impossible for any individual to attain.

From whose perspective is the preacher to speak, if not his or her own? How is the preacher to connect with the community that gathers to worship, if not through the network of human experiences we hold in common?

The life-world of the preacher, his or her experiences with the world of the scriptures and the world of the community, will shape both the content and delivery of the sermon. As we preachers stand to speak, our own self-understanding, or lack thereof, will be disclosed in our sermons, whether we intend to reveal ourselves or not.

Whether our congregations perceive us as being authentic in our preaching will depend upon the congruence between the person who is disclosed in our sermons and the person they experience us to be in our daily lives. If those two realms do not fit, we will be perceived to be among those who do not practice what we preach.

When the life-world of the preacher is viewed as one of the crucial elements in preaching, then all our experiences become resources as we approach the preaching task. That does not mean we tell everything that happens to us. It does mean that the experiences that opened a door into the world of the scripture for us might just open a door for our listeners, as well. As we begin to disclose ourselves and our journeys, we open the possibility of moving beyond being a role—the pastor—and take a step toward becoming a flesh and blood human being. As we disclose with honesty and compassion our own common humanity, our words take on the quality of shared experience with those who listen.

An additional advantage to revealing this personal life-world is the congruence that takes place between the inner world of remembrance and the outer world of daily life. In sharing the concrete world of remembrance from the preacher's life, the congregation begins to learn the idiom of the preacher, to adapt Hopewell's phrase. This "fit" between the inner life, traditionally called spirituality, and the behavior of the pastor, is perceived in the pulpit and out. It is this congruence that gives authority to preaching rather than some special knowledge or pseudo-objective vantage point.

The congruence between the inner and outer worlds of the preacher will be perceived, by those who listen, as authenticity on the part of the preacher. The listener will have a sense that the preacher truly does practice what he or she preaches. This sense of authenticity lends a trustworthiness to the preacher and the sermon.

Such trust is basic to communication and cannot be faked for very long. This trust is the common human connection that allows the hearer to say, "The preacher really knows (intimately—in the biblical sense) and believes (lives—not just professes in words) what the sermon says."

Obviously these three worlds—of the scripture, the community, and the preacher—are not discrete and separate. There are large arenas of life in which they overlap. These areas can be viewed concretely in the diagram on page 14.

Between the LIFE-WORLD OF THE SCRIPTURE and the LIFE-WORLD OF THE PREACHER is an area that contains all that pastor's previous encounters with and understandings of scripture. No preacher can ignore this backlog of assumptions and experiences based on many encounters with a number of passages of scripture when he or she sits down to prepare to preach from a specific passage.

Is the Bible a book of philosophy or practical advice, a collection of answers or stories? Do we encounter truth or God or the reflections about both from ancient cultures when we open the scriptures? What have I heard about this particular passage of scripture in sermons, in church school, or in seminary? Are the actual words of the text the Word of God or do they witness to God's Word, spoken at creation and embodied in Jesus Christ? All these questions and their answers will shape the approach a preacher takes in preparing to preach week by week.

Each person who approaches the scripture, for whatever reason, brings such a pre-understanding to the text. As hard as we may try, none of us (even those outside the church) approaches the Bible as if we had never seen or heard of it before. This is as true for the preacher as it is for each member of the congregation.

The area shared by the LIFE-WORLD OF THE SCRIPTURE and the LIFE-WORLD OF THE COMMUNITY is composed of those same preunderstandings of scripture and the sermon that the laity bring to any sermon. This is not, for most of those listening, the first time they have ever heard a sermon on scripture. Is this what I expect a sermon to be? Do I expect it to explain or inspire, to raise questions or answer them, to lead me to a decision about what I must do or tell me what I should do? Does the sermon include the scripture in a way I understand? Does the sermon reflect my current understanding of the nature of scripture.

In what contexts have the members of the congregation heard the Bible interpreted before? Are their impressions the result of intense study of the scripture in organized classes—often there are well-trained interpreters of scripture listening to sermons. Or did some of your listeners last study their Bible in a third or fourth grade Sunday school class? Do their values in interpretation come from their own training in the sciences or the humanities or from television evangelists and Bible teachers?

The listeners' previous understanding of and experience with the Bible will shape their experience of the sermon to a greater extent than most preachers know or are willing to admit.

The third area of overlapping concern lies between the LIFE-WORLD OF THE PREACHER and the LIFE-WORLD OF THE COMMUNITY. The interaction between these two arenas of experience is grounded in the mutual pre-understanding that preacher and listener bring to the event of the sermon.

Most preachers imagine an audience throughout the time the sermon is developing. Sometimes that experience includes the questions and issues that the preacher has experienced as important to that particular congregation. It may mean that the preacher imagines certain congregational members, their faces reflecting needs and responses, as the sermon is being prepared.

A sermon, a singular event of preaching, is always a once-and-for-all experience in that it speaks in a specific moment in time to a particular group of persons and their present situation. This is why books of sermons intended for cribbing are worse than useless. They deny the preacher's possibility of life-transforming encounter with the scripture, and they deny the particularity of the community into which that word is spoken. The preacher's image of the congregation in which the sermon is to be spoken will shape both the idiom and the imagery, the language and the structure of the sermon.

On the other hand, the listener's preconception of the preacher is equally important. Is this speaker to be trusted? Are the preacher's words consistent with the preacher's demeanor and actions? Do I believe the preacher believes what she or he is saying? Is it important to the preacher? Has the preacher disclosed himself or herself to me in honest and meaningful ways? Ernest Fremont Tittle was a pacifist and pastor for many years at First United Methodist Church, Evanston, Illinois. Once, a relative of one of the congregation at that church criticized Tittle's views, accused him of being unpatriotic, and suggested that he be removed from the pulpit. Tittle's parishioner suggested that the relative watch his accusations toward Tittle, who had stayed throughout the night at the bedside of the parishioner's wife as she lay dying.

Both the preconceptions of the preacher of the congregation and the listeners to the preacher figure largely in the event we call preaching.

At the very center of the three worlds lies a triangle. This is the place where the LIFE-WORLD OF THE SCRIPTURE, the LIFE-WORLD OF THE COMMUNITY, and the LIFE-WORLD OF THE

PREACHER, as well as their areas of shared concern, converge. At first glance it would seem that this triangle is the place where the sermon resides, and in part this is true. When our preaching is at its best, there is a convergence and balancing of all these worlds.

In a larger sense, that triangle of convergence is the place where all three worlds point to the presence of God. Perhaps this is the primary role of the sermon in my view of preaching, to point to the places where God is present in each world as it points all three worlds to the presence of God who transcends all worlds.

1 Gerhard von Rad, *Biblical Interpretation in Preaching*, trans. by John E. Steely (Nashville: Abingdon, 1977), p. 17.
2. James F. Hopewell, "Congregation," *Books and Religion*, Fall 1987, p. 16.
3. Ibid.

Chapter 3
JUGGLERS

The preacher is often described as a person who stands, as John Stott puts it, "between two worlds." There is a frequently repeated image ascribed to Karl Barth that the preacher is one who holds the Bible under one arm and the newspaper under the other. It is clear that the preacher is one who does not have the luxury of living in either the times of the Bible or the present age but must constantly journey from one to the other and back again.

As outlined in the last chapter, it may be even more helpful to envision preaching as taking place at the intersection of three worlds: the life-world of the scripture, the life-world of the hearer, and the life-world of the preacher. In this vision preaching is not simply a journeying back and forth between two worlds. Rather the preacher must actively balance all three worlds at the same time, giving emphasis to one or the other at a particular moment.

While both Stott and Barth are on the right track, it seems that both their images are too static. We seek a much more dynamic, dare I suggest dangerous, image of the act of preaching. We discover such an image in a tale from the folk tradition of the French.

Once there was a boy who, orphaned at an early age, was left to make his way alone through the world. He happened to fall in with a group of traveling entertainers. There he learned to juggle, to help pay his way through the world, but he still felt all alone. He was a popular part of the traveling show and did quite well when the money was collected from those who stopped to watch. But he still felt all alone in the world.

One day he was juggling when several strangers dressed in brown robes stopped to watch. One of them, a rather portly fellow, seemed to enjoy the show more than the others, especially the boy's juggling. The juggler heard the men call each other brother this and brother that, and he wondered if they truly were brothers. How lucky they were to have a family, not to be alone in the world.

After he had finished juggling, the portly brother approached the boy and told him what a fine and wondrous job he had done. The boy took that opportunity to ask if they were truly brothers. His admirer laughed and said that they were members of the same family, God's family, and that the boy was a member, too.

A family! He was a member of the family. The boy had never heard those words before. His new friend invited the juggler to return to their home with them and he too could be called brother. Since the young juggler was leaving the show, the other members of the troupe decided they would divide his earnings. He was sent away with nothing but the clothes on his back and his juggling balls.

As the monks and the young juggler were about to enter the monastery where the brothers lived, the one who had invited him to join them said, "You had best rid yourself of those. Our abbot is a solemn sort and would not take kindly to such goings on as juggling."

The boy hid his juggling balls in the hollow of a tree nearby and ran to catch up with his newfound family. He lived in the monastery, cleaning up after the other brothers to earn his bed and meals. He attended the numerous services of worship throughout the long days. And he was happy, for at last he had a family.

In the chapel where the brothers worshiped, there was a statue of Our Lady holding the baby Jesus. But something about the statue puzzled the boy. Both Mother and Son looked so terribly sad, as if together they bore the sorrows of the whole world. Often the boy thought that he would give anything to make them smile for, after all, they were family, too.

As the Feast of the Nativity came near, all the brothers were busy making gifts to take to Our Lady and the Child. Each brought the finest example of his art or craft; the farmers their vegetables and the bakers their bread. For the first time since he came to live with his new family, the boy was sad. He had nothing to offer to the Holy Mother and Child. He did not even know the special songs and prayers that would be spoken and sung on that special day.

Finally, the feast day came and all the brothers brought their gifts to the Madonna and Child, all except the boy. Following the service, after everyone else had gone, the boy had an idea. He went to the hollow tree where he had hidden his juggling balls months before and brought them to the chapel. Looking up into the sad eyes of the Lady and her small Son, the boy spoke, "I have nothing else to offer. It's all I know how to do other than sweep and wash dishes. But tonight I will juggle for you."

So the little juggler began to juggle, first one ball, then another, then a third. Soon the colored balls were arching in rainbow fashion above his head. Just then, the abbot passed the chapel and when he saw what the boy was doing he shouted "Stop! Stop immediately. What do you think you're doing?"

The boy dropped his juggling balls at the sound of the abbot's voice. The abbot came to the boy and grabbed him by the ear. The little juggler let out a yelp and the other brothers gathered to see what was happening. Just as the abbot was pulling the boy toward the door, the portly brother who had first befriended him shouted "Look!" and pointed toward the statue.

Everyone turned to look, and when they did, the sight they saw amazed them. Both the faces of Our Lady and the child Jesus had changed. They were both smiling.

Some tellers say that the little juggler was not only allowed to juggle again, but that he taught the other members of his family to juggle. And when they juggle, it is not for the applause of a crowd but for Our Lady and the Child. And to this day they smile.

This story suggests that the preacher might be viewed as a juggler attempting a form of three-ball (or three-world) juggling. Anyone who has learned even the rudiments of this art knows that you begin to learn to juggle with one ball. Once the prospective juggler has mastered the throw with one, another ball is added. This simply involves an exchange of balls from one hand to another. Then the learner makes a quantum leap by adding a third ball. To keep the balls moving in a constant pattern requires that one ball be in the air while one hand catches and one hand throws. Juggling takes intense concentration and frequent practice.

The preacher who is attempting to manage the three worlds of preaching must be a juggler. It is not enough to dash from the Bible to the newspaper or vice versa. Preaching, in this view, is not a constant running to and fro. Rather, it takes place along the journey of a preacher's life. This is the journey that counts, the pilgrimage toward maturity, mastery, and excellence.

Like the juggler, the preacher always begins with one of the worlds. The juggler does not throw all three balls up in the air at once. No, one toss begins the process, although the other two become involved very quickly. Just so, the preacher begins either in an encounter with the world of a particular passage of scripture, events of the church, community, nation, or world, or in some arena of concern for that preacher.

It is never sufficient to juggle only one ball. The preacher brings the other two worlds into play very soon after the first world is engaged. Sometimes a juggler will toss one ball higher than the other two in order to feature the green ball, say, over the red and the blue. In a similar fashion the preacher may emphasize one world in one sermon and another the following week. But all three are present in the event we call preaching.

As in the story, we do not juggle alone but invite those who listen to enter into the play as well. The little juggler in the story gave up performing for an audience to offer his gift to Our Lady and Jesus. This may help to remind us that we are not preachers/jugglers performing for a congregation/audience. No, to paraphrase Kierkegaard's reminder to us, both preacher and congregation offer our juggling of worlds to God, our Creator, who juggles the constellations we view in the night sky.

If the image of the juggler is difficult to apply to yourself, find some other activity that requires the balancing of three objects, or the use of three skills at the same time. One friend suggested that wind surfing was a more adequate image for her because it required the balancing of three planes to stay upright and move ahead. Another suggested flying a small plane was helpful because it too requires attention to the vertical, horizontal, and forward moving action of the plane.

I do not know firsthand about either of these activities, though I know that each takes time and effort to learn. Each has the advantage of moving ahead. If none of these activities embodies for you the precarious and wondrous sense of preaching, choose something from your own life experience that does.

Inventory

The following series of questions is devised to allow a pastor to take an inventory of his or her own preaching. In other words, this inventory is for your use and growth. The questions are divided into three areas, roughly analogous to the phases of preparation, delivery, and response when creating a preaching event.

These questions are deceptively simple on the surface. Yet if they are answered directly and honestly, they will lead you to a greater understanding of the process which brings you to the preaching. The answers may simply confirm what you already know about your approach to preaching. On the other hand, they may reveal to you some aspects of your journey toward excellence which had been hidden, ignored, or simply taken for granted.

This is a self-scored inventory which may allow you to think clearly and creatively about the approach to preaching that you are presently using, and it may illuminate some of the possibilities for your future preaching. Its results will assist you in making decisions about that future. Will you remain in the pattern you are presently using or will you shift to another approach, one more compatible with your present understanding of the task of preaching as it relates to you personally? Most important, allow the questions to provide for you a personal time of self-examination.

Remember that Section I of the questionnaire is intended to explore the preparatory stage of preaching. Section II includes questions that refer to the sermon itself. And Section III is intended to help you articulate the kinds of responses you expect from your preaching.

I. AND SO I BEGIN

a. I prepare to preach by using a lectionary.

always   frequently   sometimes   never

b. I prepare to preach by choosing an entire book of the Bible to preach through.

always   frequently   sometimes   never

c. I prepare to preach by choosing scriptures week by week from different places in the scripture.

always   frequently   sometimes   never

d. I prepare to preach by targeting an event or issue present in the congregation.

always   frequently   sometimes   never

e. I prepare to preach by targeting an event or issue present in the community.

always   frequently   sometimes   never

f. I prepare to preach by targeting an event or issue present in the nation or world.

always   frequently   sometimes   never

g. I prepare to preach by targeting an event or issue present in my own life.

always   frequently   sometimes   never

h. I prepare to preach by choosing a story I find particularly meaningful.

always   frequently   sometimes   never

i. I preach by choosing an idea I want to get across.

always   frequently   sometimes   never

II. ON THE WAY

a. I pattern my sermon after the flow of the biblical text.

always   frequently   sometimes   never

b. I pattern my sermon after my method of study of the biblical text.

always   frequently   sometimes   never

c. I pattern my sermon after principles derived from the biblical text.

always   frequently   sometimes   never

d. I preach to meet needs perceived in the congregation.

always   frequently   sometimes   never

e. I preach to meet needs perceived in the community.

always   frequently   sometimes   never

f. I preach to meet needs perceived in the nation or world.

always   frequently   sometimes   never

g. I draw upon my theological training as I prepare to preach.

always   frequently   sometimes   never

h. I draw upon my personal experiences as I prepare to preach.

always   frequently   sometimes   never

i. I draw upon the experiences of others as I prepare to preach.

always   frequently   sometimes   never

III. LOOKING AHEAD

a. The goal of my preaching is for the congregation to learn more about the characters and stories of the Bible.

always   frequently   sometimes   never

b. The goal of my preaching is that the congregation will learn biblical principles which apply to their lives.

always   frequently   sometimes   never

c. The goal of my preaching is that the congregation should experience the grace/judgment of God.

always   frequently   sometimes   never

d. The goal of my preaching is that persons will think differently.

always   frequently   sometimes   never

e. The goal of my preaching is that persons will feel differently.

always   frequently   sometimes   never

f. The goal of my preaching is that persons will act differently.

always   frequently   sometimes   never

g. The goal of my preaching is that I will become a vehicle of knowledge.

always   frequently   sometimes   never

h. The goal of my preaching is that I will become a vehicle of grace/judgment.

always   frequently   sometimes   never

i. The goal of my preaching is that I become a vehicle motivation to change persons' behavior.

always   frequently   sometimes   never

You will score the questions section by section. In each section there will be three blank spaces labeled

1 _____   2 _____   3 _____

Space 1 is intended for the score of the first three questions of each section, space two for the score of the second three, and space three for the score of the third group of three questions. Each response has been assigned a number thus:

always—3
frequently—2
sometimes—1
never—0

Add the total of the three questions in each section according to the answer you marked. The following chapter will outline some of the characteristics of the various approaches.

YOUR SCORE

Section I   A   B   C
1 _____   2 _____   3 _____

Section II
1 _____   2 _____   3 _____

Section III
1 _____   2 _____   3 _____

This questionnaire may be read two ways. If you read across the page, the answers in Section I will suggest whether you emphasize A. The Life-World of the Scripture, B. The Life-World of the Community, or C. The Life-World of the Preacher, as you prepare to preach. Section II will suggest your emphasis during the sermon itself (A. Scripture, B. Community, C. Preacher), and Section III will reflect which life-world is emphasized in the responses you expect from your listeners (again, A. Scripture, B. Community, or C. Preacher). Do you emphasize the same life-world throughout the process or does the emphasis change?

If you choose to read the results up and down the page, they will reflect the balance of your use of the three worlds in your week-by-week preaching. Do you focus on one more than the others? Did you realize that emphasis before you answered these questions?

Are you pleased with that emphasis or would you rather pay more attention to another of the worlds, or even attempt to balance them in your preaching each week? These are questions that will assist you in determining how you wish to continue your growth toward maturity in preaching.

The six types of preachers listed in the following chapter are intended to assist you in characterizing the kind of preaching you do now and choosing the preacher you feel called to be in the future. Remember, these types certainly do not represent the entire range of preaching types which are being practiced today, nor are they entirely separate from each other. You may find that you combine aspects of several types in your own preaching or represent a type not listed here. Nevertheless, these types which are offered should help you choose how your preaching is characterized.

Chapter 4
PILGRIMS

This chapter is intended to assist you in two ways. First, perhaps you have come to a fuller self-consciousness of your own approach to preaching through reading the previous chapters and completing the self-inventory in the last chapter. Now is the time to make some decisions based on that knowledge. The first function of this chapter is to lead you through preparations for making those decisions.

Second, this chapter will provide a number of images of the preacher to assist in decision making. Just as Chaucer's band of pilgrims included a variety of personalities, so our journey toward excellence, maturity, and mastery is populated by a diverse cast of characters. Here you will find a description of six of those character types, all of whom are represented by preachers most of us will recognize immediately. While this list is not exhaustive, these six will provide you with sufficient information to begin to make some decisions about the image of the preacher that you carry with you. This varied group of preacherly pilgrims might even include one (or more) that resembles you or me.

Decision

First, the decision is up to you. You have taken the self-inventory and discovered which of the three worlds of preaching is featured most prominently in your preparation and delivery of sermons. So what? What difference will this knowledge make in your preaching in the future?

Our approach to preaching depends heavily on the image of the preacher which we bring with us to the task. Most of us learned in seminary or by observing other preachers both a procedure for preparing sermons and a role or roles that the preacher should fulfill. Both of these elements are important to the image of the preacher each of us brings to the task of sermon preparation.

In some cases we learned who the preacher is supposed to be and how the preacher should prepare in the seminary classroom. Often, if we grew up attending church services, that image was established by those preachers who held our attention (as well as those who did not) while we were children and youth. This collection of practices and impressions which makes up our image of the preacher is certainly subject to change when we arrive in a church setting, where we are expected to preach weekly.

This change is not always easy. Change can take place intentionally or simply from neglect. Either way, changes in our preparation for and presentation of sermons are frequently accompanied by a sense of betrayal of that seminary professor or influential preacher who first set us on the path from which we are now departing.

Choice

There are three potential responses to any preacher's self-image and current approach to preaching. All three are legitimate responses. The value of the process of self-examination and self-discovery through which this book attempts to lead the reader is that the choices are intentional, that the pastor makes a choice, and follows through on that choice.

The three choices are:

1. To continue to approach preaching in essentially the same way and to bring to the task the same image of the preacher that the pastor currently holds. The response here is to simply grow and deepen along the path that one has already learned, chosen, or inherited.

2. To decide that the present approach and image of the preacher are not suitable to the pastor's sense of personhood or current situation in ministry. Then one could decide to pursue a different approach to preaching and image of the preacher. The task then is to grow and deepen that new path toward excellence.

3. To choose among the variety of images and approaches which are the most suitable to his or her gifts, understanding of scripture, and present situation in ministry. There are certain persons who have such diverse gifts and such eclectic interests that they would feel confined if limited to only one approach to preaching and image of the preacher.

The remainder of the present chapter will be devoted to descriptions of six images of the preacher. Each image of the preacher will include a description of that preacher's approach to preparation of the sermon, the primary interest, the primary tools, the primary questions, as well as a list of strengths and weaknesses of each type of preacher.

Each of the six images of the preacher stresses a specific approach to one of the three worlds of preaching. Again, these are not exhaustive of the various images of the preacher. Rather they represent the range of possible images and suggest other possibilities.

The six images of the preacher described here are:

Life-world	Type
scriptures	THE SCHOLAR THE TOUR GUIDE
community	THE MORALIST THE COMMUNITY ORGANIZER
preacher	THE COUNSELOR THE VISIONARY

The Scholar

The Scholar's Approach

The scholar is one of the two types of preacher who emphasize the life-world of the scripture. This preacher usually knows both Greek and Hebrew, and attempts to put that knowledge to good use. The scholar will spend hours poring over the lesson or lessons for the week in the original languages, comparing English translations, and doing word studies. This preacher's exegesis is thorough and usually completed early in the process of preparation.

Primary Interest

The scholar's primary interest is in biblical theology. What insights can be gained from a close and exact reading of the text? Do these fit into traditional theological categories? Does the thinking behind the text exhibit a particular stage in human understanding of God? How can the text be restated so that thinking people today can understand it?

Primary Tools

While the scholar will consult many learned commentaries and use a variety of tools, this type's main tool is the intellect and the main approach to both the content and structure of the sermon is an intellectual and rational one. Usually the sermon will be intended to persuade by logical argument and the presentation of evidence. The language will tend to be propositional, with illustrative material chosen to make the abstract language of the propositions more concrete and accessible to those listening.

Primary Questions

The primary question to which the scholar's work is addressed is, "What is the meaning of the scripture text of today's sermon?" A second question that arises for the scholar related to presentation of the sermon is, "How can I state the insights that I have gained into the meaning of the text so that my listeners can take that meaning home?"

Strengths

There are numerous strengths of the scholar's approach to preaching. The first of these is that it takes the biblical text seriously and looks at it closely. The scholar examines the language, as well as the historical and theological assumptions at work in the text. The text's meaning in its original context is honored by the scholar's approach.

A second strength is that the scholar raises the larger questions of theological meaning. Is this text speaking of grace or judgment, of the nature of God or the nature of persons, of some ancient cosmology or a meaning that speaks across the ages? These are all important issues for the scholar.

Third, the scholar's preaching usually engages the intellect of the listeners and encourages them to think. Members of the congregation will often respond with phrases such as, "I never thought of it that way before." And, "I didn't realize the scripture was referring to that." In listening to critical thinking about the Bible, the congregation can be invited to take part in their own critical reflection as a part of their personal reading of scripture and in Bible studies.

Weaknesses

Each approach to preaching has its own particular weaknesses. Often, as in life, these are directly related to the strengths of the approach. The first weakness of the scholar's approach is that its propositions often seem dry and lifeless. It can become a lecture on biblical language, history, or theology, rather than an encounter with the biblical text that has benefited by gleaning insights from those arenas of scholarship.

A second weakness of the scholar's preaching is that the language can become so abstract that it seems to lose connection to real life. The scholar's sermon runs the risk of becoming more philosophy than proclamation. Something important is missing if our response to the Good News is reduced to assenting to certain philosophical stances.

Third, since it is so concerned with the biblical text, the scholar's approach may find it more convenient to remain in the past and never make it to the present time. The issues raised by the text may seem distant unless they are translated into words and images that speak today. Fosdick poked a bit of fun at this weakness, when he referred to some preachers who assume that their congregational members are burning to know whatever happened to the Jebusites.

The Tour Guide

The Tour Guide's Approach

The second type of preacher who emphasizes the life-world of the scripture can be called the Tour Guide. This person has most likely traveled to the "Holy Land." Again, this experience shapes the approach, language, and imagery of sermons which the hearers are not likely to forget. The tour guide takes the scriptural text(s) for the week with a seriousness equal to that of the scholar, at the same time putting the text to a very different use. The tour guide's study of scripture focuses upon concrete events, persons, and attitudes which the text reflects.

Primary Interests

The Tour Guide's primary interest is to allow the listeners to experience the world of the scripture text. The sermon is an introduction to the persons, sights, and sounds of that world. The Tour Guide leads the listeners through the world of the text by pointing out to them significant features of that landscape and characters in that world. Who are these people? Why do they perform the actions and say the words recorded in the text? Who spoke the text originally? To whom was it spoken? What was the attitude of the speaker and listeners? Why was it remembered?

Primary Tools

The Tour Guide will look for help more toward Bible diction-
aries and descriptions of biblical archeology and life in ancient
times than to traditional theological commentaries. Studies in
narrative and poetic form and content of the Bible will hold special
interest for this type of preacher. The primary tool of the Tour
Guide, though, is the imagination. It is through an imaginative
entry to the world of the text that this preacher discovers the
sermon. And the appeal of this person's preaching is usually to the
imaginations of those sitting in the congregation. The Tour Guide's
language will include concrete descriptions of people and places,
as well as reflect the feelings and attitudes of narrator and characters in the text.

Primary Questions

The primary question that informs the Tour Guide's preparation to preach is, "What should the listener experience of the world
of the text?" The answer will include the background information
needed to flesh out the text: What was happening in the church at
Corinth and prompting Paul's response? What were the marriage
customs at the time of Jesus' birth? How were shepherds, or
soldiers, or tax collectors viewed at the time? The quest to answer
such questions gives shape to the study that contributes to the
Tour Guide's preaching, and the answers provide content and
suggest forms for the sermon.

Strengths

The strengths of the Tour Guide's approach to preaching are
related to its imaginative quality. First, it leads both preacher and
listeners to encounter scripture through their imaginations. A
sense of place and kinship is nurtured as we participate in those
biblical worlds. Our knowledge is concrete rather than abstract;
there is a sense of reality which leads the listener to believe that

one could almost reach out and touch the people, places, and things of the sermon. The stories, poems, and letters then have a life of their own in the imagination of the community as it continues its journey of faith.

A second strength of this approach is that its power is grounded in the experience of the preacher and congregation. In the sermon we meet the people, see the sights and hear the sounds of the biblical world. Our knowledge is not simply intellectual but experiential. Such encounters with the scripture tend to encourage enthusiasm for study of the times of the Bible; their history, customs, and beliefs. We come to view biblical characters as people who have the same strengths and weaknesses, joys and sorrows as we have. Through sharing such experiences, the preacher and congregation begin to include their forebears as companions on the journey of faith.

The third strength is that each listener is allowed to interpret the experience of the biblical world based upon her or his own needs and understanding. While every sermon, even one that recounts a biblical narrative, is an interpretation, there is usually no authoritative word given concerning the insights everyone should take away from the sermon. Such an approach acknowledges that there is a variety of meanings and interpretations which can emerge from an encounter with a single biblical world. In a sense, the Tour Guide allows the community to become the interpreter of scripture, not the preacher alone.

Weaknesses

The weaknesses of the Tour Guide's approach to preaching are, again, related to its strengths. First, the Tour Guide's sermon will rarely fit the expectations of someone coming to hear a rational, logical presentation of insights. It will seem interesting, even entertaining, but sadly lacking in both structure and substance. "Where were your points?" an incisive member may ask. "What message was I supposed to get out of it?" Such questioners will rarely be satisfied with the response, "Well, what do you think you were supposed to get out of it?"

A second weakness to which this approach may fall victim is

that it simply may leave certain listeners confused. They know that you added a great deal of information to the passage of scripture, but is it "true" or did you just make it up? If this leads me to a new understanding of a story, psalm, letter, or prophetic utterance, how do I square this new interpretation with the understanding I brought with me to the sermon? Such confusion and conflicted feelings could lead to that person's simply dismissing the sermon altogether.

Third, some listeners may not feel capable of applying their experience of the biblical world to their daily lives. They will ask, "So, what does this have to do with me?" If the application is left up to the listener, some in the congregation will assume that, while interesting, the sermon really has no effect on the way they live their lives or relate to their family members or co-workers. If this is not a source of frustration, then the sermon becomes simply one more form of entertainment.

While both the Scholar and the Tour Guide focus on the life world of the scriptures, the ways they deal with the world in shaping both their preparation for preaching and the actual event of the sermon are vastly different.

The Moralist

The Moralist's Approach

This is one of two images of the preacher that stress the life-world of the community as the basic motivating force behind their preaching. The Moralist begins with a concern for the individual needs of congregational members, especially those related to making ethical choices. These may relate to issues as various as the use of alcohol or tobacco, military service, consumption of boycotted grapes or lettuce, and business or sexual ethics. For the Moralist, the Bible and the tradition inherited from the larger historic community of faith provide guidance in making such choices. This type of preacher will be very discerning of the pressures and ambiguities involved in decision making and will attempt to assist persons hearing the sermon to clarify that process. For the Moralist, the scripture is a record of the struggle of people to make faithful decisions, their successes and failures. Thus it can be of help to us in that same struggle.

Primary Interest

The primary interest of the Moralist is to encourage persons to relate their personal ethical decisions to their faith and the faith tradition. The quality of our lives is our most telling witness in this view, and the Moralist's preaching aims to improve that quality wherever possible. What kind of person am I called by God to be? How can I make decisions that are consistent with what I believe? How does my behavior witness for or against my faith? How do I relate to persons whose values are different from my own?

Primary Tools

The Moralist will draw upon moral philosophy, traditional values, sociological studies and statistics, as well as the Bible in appealing to the will of listeners. The Moralist will include examples of virtue, rational arguments, appeals to the common good and the good of the individual, or all of these in preaching. The sermon will often target a specific behavior or group of behaviors and relate these to the witness of the Bible and the Christian tradition. These may focus on conflicts or relationships within the congregation, in relation to one's participation in the larger community, or help shape one's response as a citizen of a particular nation or the world.

Primary Question

The question that would have a primary place in the Moralist's preparation is, "How will my preaching encourage and assist those who hear to make personal ethical decisions that are consistent with the biblical witness, the Christian tradition, and the person's own faith?" The Moralist is more concerned with raising issues and providing criteria and procedures for decision making than in offering cut and dried answers. This preacher hopes both to challenge and encourage those who face decisions concerning their personal behavior every day.

Strengths

It is unfortunate that the title, Moralist, has become a rather negative designation in recent times. A concern for the good, and ethical decision making based upon that good, have long been a part of the religious and philosophic traditions of both East and West. The Moralist exhibits at least three strengths as a preacher.

First, the Moralist engages listeners in their role as decision makers. Philosophers of the past call this faculty the Will. This preacher helps the congregation to know the extent of their own freedom to make decisions and encourages them to consider the impact of those decisions carefully. For the Moralist we are individuals with the free will to choose the creative or destructive paths in life, and we are called to take responsibility for those choices.

Second, the Moralist offers ethical insights to assist in making those important decisions. By drawing from the Bible, from accepted standards of morality, and from studies in decision making, this preacher seeks to provide a framework within which one can live a life consistent with one's beliefs. The response the Moralist invites is an active decision and changed behavior. We are not simply persons who can think or feel. We are persons who perform actions. The Moralist is concerned that these actions be examined and changed, if needed.

Third, the preaching of the Moralist emphasizes personal morality. This is not as individualistic an approach as it may seem at first. It is clear for this preacher that our choices and actions affect other people: friends, family, the congregation, and the community. Thus the Moralist will emphasize the responsibility of ethical decision making in our relationships. The most important outcome for this approach is that people not simply be good by accepted standards. Rather, the Moralist calls the listeners to be faithful to God and their neighbors and understands that such faithfulness is reflected in choices and behaviors.

Weaknesses

Among the weaknesses of the Moralist's approach to preaching is, first, that an answer for every dilemma in life is implied. The Bible is scoured for specific answers to specific situations in which decisions are called for. The implication that there is one and only one right choice in a given situation simply does not square with many listeners' experience of the scripture or of their daily lives. Perhaps the most dangerous extreme of this view occurs when the preacher is set up as the person with all the answers, the one who can speak with authority on the decisions everyone should make.

A second weakness is that the Moralist's worldview can tend to divide every event into good and evil categories. Sometimes this division of the world also colors the preacher's view of persons. People, too, can be divided into the good (those who agree with the preacher's ethical views) and the evil (those who take another view). While it may be true that no act is morally neutral, persons as actors in the world make decisions and behave in ways that include a mixture of motives as well as effects. The temptation here is to make the division between creative and destructive actions too clear, to define the arenas of good and evil so distinctly that there is no room for the ambiguity that is always present in human decision making.

Third, in a quest for ethical clarity, the Moralist may obscure the Mystery that lies at the heart of faith. Those who attempt to do good suffer and those who seem to care nothing for ethical life prosper. God makes the rain to fall on the just and the unjust alike. Faith is not simply a matter of ethics in a universe in which God can choose a Jacob or a David with all their moral failures as divine instruments. Even human choice is not clearcut. As St. Paul puts it, we do those things we do not wish to do and we refuse to do the right thing even when we know it is right. To deny the Mystery that lies at the heart of God and the tradition of the church is to reduce a living and growing faith to nothing more than a series of do's and don't's.

The Community Organizer

The Community Organizer's Approach

The second type of preacher who stresses the life-world of the community is the Community Organizer. While the Moralist tends to emphasize personal ethics, the Community Organizer will focus attention on corporate ethical decision making. This preacher will raise issues related to economics, peace, and justice. These controversies may take the form of local referenda on economic or social issues; discrimination against persons based on race, sex, age, or physical condition; national policy related to homeless persons; human rights abroad or at home; or a variety of other issues. The Community Organizer's concern for these issues emerges from the call for justice in the scriptures, especially the prophets and certain sayings and stories of Jesus. The sermon in this view is a call to action, a call for a transformed community—the church—to transform the world.

Primary Interest

The primary interest of the Community Organizer is to move people to examine their faith, by relating it to their lives in such a fashion that they begin to see their own participation in the evil and destructive structures of the world, and then take steps to reduce that participation. How does my standard of living affect those living among the poor in my own country and around the world? Do the products I purchase contribute to the exploitation of workers anywhere in the world? How do decisions made by my government (local, state, national) affect the lives of persons here and abroad, especially the powerless. How does my faith shape the decisions made by me and those who represent me as they touch the lives of the least of my sisters and brothers? These are questions that significantly influence the preaching of the Community Organizer.

Primary Tools

The Community Organizer keeps up very carefully on the news of the day, following the reports of both major newspapers and television news programs and the responses of religious and alternative media for help with interpreting world events. This preacher is usually grounded in the scripture with its concern for the stranger, the outcast, the widow, and the orphan. Often this preacher will include sociological, political, and economic analysis of both the biblical and modern world in preparing to preach.

Primary Questions

The Community Organizer's foremost question related to preaching is, "How will my preaching empower persons to examine their faith and life choices as they relate to the scriptural call to justice and as they affect the lives of others in the community, nation, and world?" This approach will be concerned with the vast range of public morality issues, including individual decisions (from horse or dog racing to paying war taxes), corporate decisions (the community of faith's response to abortion, housing for the homeless, or nuclear weapons), and national decisions (including world distribution of food, human rights, or the sale of weapons). Here again, the emphasis is on making decisions that reflect one's faith as fully as possible.

Strengths

The strengths of the approach to preaching characteristic of the Community Organizer are numerous. First, this approach stresses decision making and appeals to the will, a strength shared with the Moralist. The Community Organizer expects that the reflections on faith and life which are encouraged by the sermon, will lead to decisions and actions. Here the basic understanding is that our actions speak louder than words and that our best witness is a life devoted to a biblical vision of shalom for all people. Preaching means empowering persons to live such a witness.

Second, the Community Organizer shifts the focus of primary concern away from the self and toward others. The welfare of the individual is inextricably tied to the welfare of others in this view. This is especially true as the choices and actions of individuals and communities affect the lives of the poor and powerless. The neighbor, even the stranger, becomes the primary focus of concern, and preaching is viewed as one significant way to make this shift in consciousness.

Third, such preaching turns attention toward meeting the needs of others rather than personal gain. It may call for intentionally giving up certain advantages so that others may have a basic quality of life. This call to sacrifice is based in a reading of prophetic passages from the Hebrew Bible, the life and teachings of Jesus as recorded in the Gospels, and a long Christian tradition of searching love. This type of preaching is concerned with putting possessions in perspective, lifting the values of a humane life above exorbitant material gain.

Weaknesses

Among the weaknesses of the Community Organizer's approach are, first, the possibility that an emphasis upon decisions and actions could lose its grounding in the scriptures and traditions that present the vision and the criteria that give shape to one's life. The preacher can find herself or himself more concerned with the practical results of a community action than its rootage in study and prayer. The danger here is that the life faithful to shalom is measured against a standard of effectiveness rather than faithfulness.

Second, another weakness related to the first is that the preaching of the Community Organizer runs the risk of becoming so concerned with the techniques of social, economic, or political change that the reasons for such change are lost. In other words, the preacher becomes so concerned with the *how* that the *why* is lost. Too great a focus on technique can produce a community of highly efficient organizers who have lost touch with both the reason for organizing and the goal toward which it originally aimed, the peace and justice that reflect God's shalom.

Third, once a community has been empowered to make decisions and take action, it too may define anyone who disagrees with that position as, at best, misguided or, at worst, evil—a demonic enemy of God and people. For the individual or community that believes their choices to be faithful ones, there is always the temptation to define any other choice as unfaithful. The weakness here is based upon the failure to keep in mind the limitations of all human decisions and actions, the impurity of all human motives, and that an absolute standpoint on the truth belongs to God alone.

The Moralist and the Community Organizer share a concern for making decisions that are consistent with the biblical witness, the tradition of the church, and one's own faith stance. They differ in that the Moralist tends to focus attention on the individual, while the Community Organizer stresses the community.

The Counselor

The Counselor's Approach

The Counselor is one of the preaching types who emphasize the life-world of the preacher in preparation and presentation of sermons. This type of preacher might best be described as the wounded healer. The counselor cannot be a totally self-absorbed person. Rather, this preacher uses insights gained through his or her own struggle with scripture and the joys and difficulties of life to assist the growth and health of others. This preacher seeks common human experiences through which to communicate hope and the possibility of change. These common human experiences might be found in the preacher's own life, in scripture, or in the lives of others.

Primary Interest

The primary interest of the Counselor is to promote growth and health in the lives of those who hear the sermon. To accomplish this, the preacher must develop a sensitivity to the needs of those who sit in the pews week after week. Listening skills must be sharpened as home, hospital, and workplace visits become a major part of preparation for preaching. Then, out of that preacher's personal experience of the members of the congregation, the issues which the sermon will address emerge. Alcohol or drug abuse, spouse or child abuse, loss of employment, divorce, unwed parenthood as they appear in the congregation become the springboard for the sermon.

Primary Tools

An obvious tool for the Counselor's preparation to preach is that preacher's autobiography. Searching one's own past for instances of common human experience and the insights they have offered to difficult life situations is both a form of spiritual formation (self-examination) and an attempt to identify with persons in the congregation. Listening to the life situations that arise within the congregation is also an essential part of this preacher's preparation. The scriptures provide stories, songs, and reflections on a variety of human situations and thus direct our attention to God's presence in those situations. The counselor may draw from the learnings of psychology, faith development, and pastoral care, as well.

Primary Question

The primary question for the preacher who functions as Counselor can be phrased, "How can I listen to my congregational members' life situations so that I can draw from personal experiences of my own life, my encounter with the scriptures, and my listening to other persons so that my sermon might speak a healing word to my listeners?" This preacher will begin with needs that he or she perceives from experience in that congregation and search for the resources to speak to those needs. The Counselor views the sermon as providing for the care and cure of souls.

Strengths

The first of the Counselor's strengths as a preacher is the ability to listen for hurts in the lives of others, whether stated explicitly or hidden beneath their words. Listening to others, one's own life, and the scriptures is the most difficult and rewarding aspect of this approach. The preaching of the Counselor engages persons at the level of their human needs, a place of potentially great healing. In this view, every experience, no matter how tragic or hurtful, can sensitize us for preaching that helps persons to bear the burdens of life.

A second strength of the Counselor is that this preacher seeks to provide a context in which the disorientation, pain, and disappointments of life can be incorporated into growth toward maturity of faith. The preacher here is not the example of the whole or complete person, but a fellow struggler on the way toward the wholeness that God intends for each person. Elements of the preacher's life are disclosed not to set the preacher apart from other persons but to offer the listener another companion on the way.

Third, the Counselor's preaching is most often received in the spirit in which it is offered, the listener thinking, "This preacher really cares about me and my difficulties. She (he) does not have all the answers but is willing to walk by my side and share insights for the healing of both of us." This kind of preaching can empower the listener to face all of life as a part of a community of caring. In addition, the Counselor models for the listener a way of listening to one's own life that works toward healing the past and wholeness for the future.

Weaknesses

Weaknesses within the Counselor's approach to preaching include, first, that it could lead to an unhealthy self-absorption on the part of the preacher or the listener. The abuses of this approach by preachers lead some teachers of preaching to suggest that it is never appropriate to draw upon one's own life experiences in the sermon. While the dangers of this approach are important to heed, an examination of one's life is to find common human experiences to assist others to examine and find resources for growth and health in their lives. This approach is not intended to become an excuse for the preacher to tell the congregation what a shining example of virtue his or her life has been, or an excuse to bleed before the congregation in an effort to gain sympathy for the preacher's circumstances.

Second, because of its concern for personal growth in faith, the Counselor's approach may depend more on popular psychology and self-help techniques than on finding its roots in the biblical and theological sources of the Christian faith. Such preaching provides not a panacea for life's difficulties but companions and guidance for the struggles that appear along life's way. Such preaching that does not provide a biblically sound context for suffering and failure is in danger of becoming just another form of "pop" psychologizing.

The third weakness of the Counselor's approach is that in its concern for personal growth, it may lack a prophetic dimension. The prophets call people to be accountable for their decisions and actions and their effects on others. If the Counselor does not look outward as well as inward, the goal of the sermon becomes little more than making people feel good about themselves. There is a time appropriate for guilt, for persons to feel bad about their participation in selfish and destructive lifestyles. Without this prophetic dimension, preaching creates communities of people who cannot see beyond their own personal needs.

The Visionary

The Visionary's Approach

The Visionary is the second of the preacher types whose energy and impetus comes from the life-world of the preacher.

This type approaches preaching based upon a perception of who her or his congregation is as the church and a vision of what its future role can be. The Visionary leads the people by projecting with them future scenarios for their lives together. Such issues as the growth of the congregation in knowledge, ministry, or numbers; the use of existing land and buildings or the development of new places of ministry; or participation with other groups to provide services for the good of the community—all interest the Visionary. This preacher's orientation is toward the future. Just as the Counselor is seeking to promote health and growth for individuals, the Visionary is promoting health and growth in the congregation as a whole.

Primary Interest

The Visionary is interested in developing a congregation of people on the way, moving into the future guided by a vision of their particular calling. If one group of people cannot do everything, what is God calling *us* to do and be in our community and world? How does the Bible provide challenges to us and role models for us to follow as we move into the future? How do I as the preacher inspire others to claim a vision of God's calling and facilitate them in realizing that vision? How do I reflect to the congregation my perceptions of them and their future directions and their gifts and graces for realizing a vision? These are all questions that hold an interest for the Visionary.

Primary Tools

The Visionary draws heavily upon his or her own experience of the congregation in assisting them to discover a vision. The Bible is a source of motivation toward growth as a community, images of possible futures, and examples of how the Hebrew and early Christian communities claimed their unique place on the way. This preacher will be on the lookout for gifts among the people to employ in this vision and will preach in ways that motivate others to claim their gifts (time, talent, money) in realizing the vision. Resources on understanding congregations, their motivation and growth, will be a part of this preacher's preparation of the sermon.

Primary Questions

The primary question that shapes the Visionary's preaching is, "How can my preaching reflect to the congregation my experience of their gifts and graces for healthy growth in faith and ministry so that they can claim a vision of who God is calling them to be in the future?" This approach will affirm strengths among the congregation, present possible futures for the congregation based on the preacher's experience of them as faithful persons, and motivate the community to come to certain decisions about their future as the church.

Strengths

The Visionary's approach to preaching affirms the gifts and graces present in a congregation, which is its first strength. The community that sees itself as gifted is likely to be sure that those gifts are not wasted. The Visionary's preaching can move the listeners beyond simply doing and allow them a glimpse of being a special community for God in service to others. From the breaking of bread in communion to the sharing of bread in a soup kitchen, a vision of who we are as God's people guides our actions.

A second strength of the Visionary is that, for this preacher, the Bible is not just a book of the past but of the future. It is not a collection of ancient advice. Rather the biblical witness provides images and models for us to follow into the future as we pursue our own calling as the church. In this view the Bible is a book whose full richness we have yet to discover.

Third, the Visionary uses her or his personal experience of the congregation as a mirror in which the listeners can view possible scenarios of their future as the church. The personal vision of the preacher as embodied in preaching becomes a form of leadership and motivation of the congregation to realize potential of which they may not be fully aware.

Weaknesses

The first weakness of the Visionary's approach is that it is constantly in danger of equating God's vision for a congregation with its own vision of itself or the preacher's vision of it. Just because we want to be someone or do something does not mean that our choice is automatically consistent with the biblical witness or God's present will for us or for the world. It is all too easy to confuse a congregation's desire to be bigger or more influential with a call from God to these things.

A second weakness, related to the first, is that the Visionary's emphasis on the future can lead to a dangerous ignorance of the past. The Bible and the past experiences of Christian communities can provide a corrective to equating our wants with God's will. While a focus on the future is an appropriate stance for Christians, we are a people with a tradition that can instruct us and help keep us faithful to God's working in the world.

Finally, since the vision of the congregation is often sparked by the personal vision of the preacher, it is easy for the pastor to impose a vision on the people that has not emerged from their own self-examination and study of the scripture. Is God calling this congregation to build a building or is that simply the pastor's desire for this church? Is the preacher devoted to ministries to the homeless and helpless, but the congregation has not been given the time, study, and prayer to claim that as their own caling? The Visionary must remember that the preacher is to lead, not impose; the calling is to the whole people of God, not just one.

The Counselor and Visionary share a concern for growth and health. While the Counselor seeks to promote the growth of individuals, the Visionary encourages the growth of communities. Each attempts to assure that such growth is grounded in the biblical witness and the Christian tradition.

* * * *

We have surveyed six types of preacher whose various approaches emerge from the three life-worlds of preaching. Again, these are not exhaustive. There are many other types of preacher, and the division could certainly be made along very different lines. You may not see yourself among the numbers of any of these preachers. Or you may see yourself functioning as one type on one occasion and another at another time.

The danger in identifying specific types is that we choose one approach and claim that it is superior to all the others for all preachers. There are excellent preachers of each type described above, and others of equal quality whose preaching defies this or any attempt to identify its type. The question is not which type is the best. Ask yourself, "Which type best describes me? Do I want to continue my present approach or change?"

Which type(s) of preacher listed above describes my current approach to preaching?

Do I wish to continue to journey toward excellence in this approach?

If I wish to make a change, in which type(s) approach am I going to grow toward excellence?

What will be my first step toward this continued growth? (The following chapter should assist you in answering this.)

Chapter 5
PEERS

Where do I go from here? Since I have made a decision about my preaching, how do I follow through on that decision? The present chapter intends to offer some suggestions, some first steps toward your continued growth in preaching.

Several years ago a group of very distinguished colleagues in ministry gathered to assist me to develop programs for assisting pastors with their preaching. Their number included a bishop, the pastor of a prominent congregation, a campus minister at an outstanding university, a pastor who also taught preaching at a seminary, and a recent seminary graduate who was pastoring a church for the first time. I asked them to describe from their observation and experience the most important forms for continued education in preaching.

Without exception the group agreed on a mutually supportive framework for preaching.

1. Learning that took place in the physical presence of *a leader who makes a presentation and interacts with the learners* was viewed as an excellent means of learning. Continuing education events that bring a preacher or teacher of preaching to present material and then allow time for open discussion, or presentations and critique by the learners, were clearly viewed as a very valuable growth experiences for preachers.

2. A second important learning experience, the group said, was to view a presentation on *videotape* and have group discussion following. Videotape preserved both the visual and audio qualities of the presentation; the only feature distinguishing it from live presentation was interaction with the presenter.

3. Third in the group's list of learning experiences was listen-

ing to an *audiotape* of a presentation followed by group discussion. The audiotape still preserves the live human voice, though both the visual aspects of the presentation and interaction with the presenter are lacking.

4. The fourth means of growth in preaching among the learning experiences listed by the group was reading and discussing *written material*. The written material is lacking live interaction with the writer, as well as both visual and auditory dimensions of the presentation.

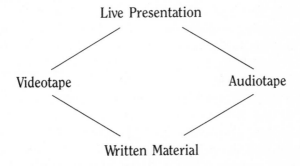

This framework of values assumed that the learning would take place within a group of learners. The discussion and plans for future growth that take place following a presentation are crucial elements in learning. Any of these activities done alone would decrease in its overall value to the learner.

As you seek to grow toward excellence, realize that you are not alone in that process. Not only is the group support and critique important to the learning of skills, your colleagues are there to support and sustain you through the plateaus in your growth. Also, there is an important theological dimension to group learning. Preaching is the responsibility of the whole church, not one preacher. As you grow toward excellence, you join hands with other preachers and the laypersons in your congregation so that the proclamation of the good news is from the whole people of God for the whole world.

To assist you in forming a colleague study group or deepening the learning experience of an existing group, see my book *Preach-*

ing Peers (order no. W132K, Nashville, Discipleship Resources, 1987). This is a guide to group study aimed toward growth in preaching. It is very practical in its suggestions and can be used with a variety of content—live presentation, videotape, audiotape, or written material—making it a very versatile resource.

Directions for Growth Toward Excellence in Preaching

1. *Live Presentation:* Since the living presence of a leader is the most direct means of continuing one's education, one step toward excellence is to register for events sponsored by seminaries or church bodies that feature one or more teachers of preaching. The dates and places of such events can be obtained through denominational or seminary publications. Three such national events related to preaching are Proclamation, sponsored by Cokesbury Seminars of the United Methodist Publishing House and the Section on Worship of the General Board of Discipleship of The United Methodist Church; The Harry Emerson Fosdick Convocation at Union Theological Seminary in New York City; and the Lyman Beecher Lectures in Preaching at Yale Divinity School. Most seminaries have alumni events which feature preaching lectures.

If you choose to form a peer study group in your local community, one option for the content of the study is live presentation of an invited leader. Perhaps you live near a seminary or university from whose faculty you would choose a leader to present your group's content. This might be a professor of biblical studies, history, or speech communication, depending on the needs and desires of your group. Or maybe there is a pastor in your area known for a particular skill related to preaching who would serve as your invited leader. The options for live presentation are many and various.

2. *Videotape:* More and more seminaries and university chapels are videotaping the sermons and lectures that are given on their campuses. Many make these tapes available on loan or for rental or purchase. Conferences, dioceses, and presbyteries have

audiovisual libraries that include videotapes on a number of subjects. Even local colleges will have videotape collections that include such subjects as religion, speech, or history which might be applicable to preaching.

If you plan a peer study group and find it impossible to engage live leadership, videotape is the next best means of instruction. If the group includes pastors from several denominations, have each participant search out the denominational or seminary collections most familiar to them. Some religious publishers have a section of their catalogue devoted to videotaped resources. Even if these must be purchased, the cost is usually not prohibitive if shared by the entire group.

Three videotaped resources you should be aware of are:

Fred Craddock, *Preaching*. Nashville: Abingdon, 1986.
The four tapes in this set provide a solid basic approach to preaching that is both biblical and imaginative.

James Forbes, *Preaching Christian Stewardship*. New York: The National Council of Churches.
These four tapes deal with one of the most important and problematic issues in preaching. A study resource, *Preaching Christian Stewardship: A Study Guide,* by Michael E. Williams is available from Discipleship Resources.

Michael E. Williams, *Storytelling: A Journey into New Worlds,* Nashville: Discipleship Resources, 1988.
This tape is an introduction to the art of storytelling for pastors, teachers, parents, or anyone else interested in learning to tell a story.

These are only three of numerous video resources that could assist a group of pastors on the journey toward excellence.

3. *Audiotape:* The third best resource material to continue one's education in preaching is found on audiotape. This is a readily available and inexpensive means of allowing the living voice of a teacher or preacher to speak to you. In a peer study group you may already have a number of resources by simply gathering those owned by the group members.

Again, a number of seminaries have collections of sermons and lectures on audiotape. Two of the most wide-ranging collections are:

The Reigner Tape Library
Union Theological Seminary
Richmond, VA 23227

and

The Listening Library
Catalog of Recordings
The Dept. of Speech
Princeton Theological Seminary
CN821
Princeton, NJ 08542

Both of these have catalogues of their holdings and offer tapes for loan or sale. Inquire if the seminary you attended or one near you has a collection of audiotapes for loan or sale.

Two audiotape series that may interest you are:

The Circuit Rider Sermon Series
The United Methodist Publishing House
201 Eighth Ave., S.
P.O. Box 801
Nashville, TN   37202

and

The Newscope Lecture Series
The United Methodist Publishing House
201 Eighth Ave., S.
P.O. Box 801
Nashville, TN   37202

The sermon series includes a sermon, comments from the preacher, and a critique from several listeners on each tape. The preachers are United Methodist and serve in a variety of locations. The lecture series collects lectures and sermons delivered in a number of settings by leaders of a variety of denominations

4. *Written Material:* Written resources are still the most readily available source for content, whether in group or individual study.

Among the written materials that assist in growth in preaching, the most important is creative literature. It is crucial for the preacher to read novels, short stories, and poems, not scanning them for sermon illustrations but to learn from them better ways to communicate through words and images. Your reading may range from classical authors to those recently published. You may choose to read from the genres of popular culture. Reading or, even better, attending plays will strengthen a preacher's sense of the sound of spoken language and the feel for dramatic moments.

This type of reading should offer you pleasure as well as shape the way you communicate. Literature cultivates the whole human being, and such wholeness is, after all, a great asset in preaching.

The following bibliography of written sources does not pretend to be exhaustive. Rather, it is selective in two senses. It includes material of a general nature related to preaching from influential and recently published writers, preachers, and teachers. Second, it collects a number of resources under the headings of the three worlds of preaching. This is done to assist each pastor in choosing the resources that will most directly promote his or her growth in the world of preaching each has chosen to emphasize. Two good sources of reviews of new publications for pastors are *Homiletic*, Lutheran School of Theology, Gettysburg, PA and *Books and Religion,* The Divinity School, Duke University, Durham, NC 27706.

General Preaching Resources

Mortimer Adler, *How to Speak/How to Listen* (New York: Macmillan, 1983).

Elizabeth Achtemeier, *Preaching as Theology and Art* (Nashville: Abingdon, 1984).

Charles Bartow, *The Preaching Moment: A Guide to Sermon Delivery* (Nashville: Abingdon, 1980).

Frederick Buechner, *Telling the Truth: The Gospel as Tragedy, Comedy and Fairy Tale* (San Francisco: Harper and Row, 1977).

Walter Burghardt, *Preaching: The Art and Craft* (New York: Paulist Press, 1987).

David Buttrick, *Homiletic: Moves and Structures* (Philadelphia: Fortress, 1987).

William J. Carl III, *Preaching Christian Doctrine* (Philadelphia: Fortress, 1984).

Fred B. Craddock, *Preaching* (Nashville: Abingdon, 1985).

_____, *As One Without Authority* (Nashville: Abingdon, 1979).

_____, *Overhearing the Gospel* (Nashville: Abingdon, 1978).

Helen Gray Crotwell, *Women and the Word: Sermons* (Philadelphia: Fortress, 1978).

Milton Crum, *Manual on Preaching* (Valley Forge: Judson, 1977).

Richard Eslinger, *A New Hearing* (Nashville: Abingdon, 1987).

Clyde E. Fant, *Preaching for Today* (New York: Harper and Row, 1975; revised edition 1987).

Richard Lischer, *A Theology of Preaching: The Dynamics of the Gospel* (Nashville: Abingdon, 1981).

Eugene Lowry, *Doing Time in the Pulpit* (Nashville: Abingdon, 1985).

_____, *The Homiletic Plot* (Atlanta: John Knox, 1983).

Edward F. Marquart, *Quest for Better Preaching* (Minneapolis: Augsburg, 1985).

Henry M. Mitchell, *The Recovery of Preaching* (New York: Harper and Row, 1977).

J. Randall Nichols, *Building the Word: The Dynamics of Communication and Preaching* (New York: Harper and Row, 1981).

Ronald E. Sleeth, *God's Word and Our Words* (Atlanta: John Knox, 1986).

John R. W. Stott, *Between Two Worlds: The Art of Preaching in the Twentieth Century* (Grand Rapids: Eerdmans, 1982).

William H. Willimon, *Preaching and Leading Worship* (Philadelphia: Westminster, 1984).

Michael E. Williams, *Preaching Peers* (Nashville: Discipleship Resources, 1987).

The Life-World of the Scripture

Walter Brueggmann, *The Message of the Psalms* (Minneapolis: Augsburg, 1984).

James W. Cox, ed., *Biblical Preaching: An Expositor's Treasury* (Philadelphia: Westminster, 1983).

Fred B. Craddock, John H. Hayes, and Carl R. Holladay, *Preaching the New Common Lectionary,* Years A, B, & C (Nashville: Abingdon, 1984-87).

John Dominic Crossan, *The Dark Interval* (Niles, IL: Argus, 1975).

Reginald H. Fuller, *Preaching the Lectionary* (Collegeville: The Liturgical Press, 1984).

_____, *The Use of the Bible in Preaching* (Philadelphia: Fortress, 1981).

Robert W. Funk, *Parables and Presence* (Philadelphia: Fortress, 1982).

Barry W. Holtz, ed., *Back to the Sources: Reading the Classic Hebrew Texts* (New York: Summit Books, 1984).

Werner H. Kelber, *The Oral and the Written Gospel: The Hermeneutics of Speaking and Writing in the Synoptic Tradition, Mark, Paul, and Q* (Philadelphia: Fortress, 1983).

Leander E. Keck, *The Bible in the Pulpit: The Renewal of Biblical Preaching* (Nashville: Abingdon, 1978).

Dennis Ronald MacDonald, *The Legend of the Apostle: The Battle for Paul in Story and Canon* (Philadelphia: Westminster, 1983).

Sallie McFague, *Speaking in Parables* (Philadelphia: Fortress, 1975).

Wayne A. Meeks, *The First Urban Christians: The Social World of the Apostle Paul* (New Haven: Yale University Press, 1983).

Gail R. O'Day, *The Word Disclosed: John's Story and Narrative Preaching* (St. Louis: CBP Press, 1987).

Daniel Patte, *Preaching Paul* (Philadelphia: Fortress, 1984).

W. Gunther Plaut, ed. *The Torah: A Modern Commentary* (New York: Union of American Hebrew Congregations, 1981).

David Rosenberg, *Congregation: Contemporary Writers Read the Jewish Bible* (New York: Harcourt, Brace, Jovanovich, 1987).

James A. Sanders, *God Has a Story Too: Biblical Sermons in Context* (Philadelphia: Fortress, 1979).

Elizabeth Schüssler Fiorenza, *Bread Not Stone: The Challenge of Feminist Biblical Interpretation* (Boston: Beacon Press, 1984).

Bernard Brandon Scott, *The Word of God in Words: Reading and Preaching* (Philadelphia: Fortress, 1985).

D. Moody Smith, *Interpreting the Gospels for Preaching* (Philadelphia: Fortress, 1980).

William D. Thompson, *Preaching Biblically: Exegesis and Interpretation* (Nashville: Abingdon, 1981).

Phyllis Trible, *God and the Rhetoric of Sexuality* (Philadelphia: Fortress, 1978).

Don W. Wardlaw, ed., *Preaching Biblically: Creating Sermons in the Shape of Scripture* (Philadelphia: Westminster, 1983).

Amos N. Wilder, *Early Christian Rhetoric: The Language of the Gospel* (Cambridge: Harvard Univ. Press, 1971).

The Life-World of the Community

Robert N. Bellah, Richard Madsen, William M. Sullivan, Ann Swindler, and Stephen Tipton, *Habits of the Heart: Individualism and Commitment in American Life* (Berkeley: University of California Press, 1986).

Robert McAfee Brown, *Unexpected News: Reading the Bible through Third World Eyes* (Philadelphia: Westminster, 1984).

Carol Gilligan, *In a Different Voice: Psychological Theory and Women's Development* (Cambridge, MA: Harvard University Press, 1982).

Justo and Catherine González, *Liberation Preaching: The Pulpit and the Oppressed* (Nashville: Abingdon, 1980).

Wesley Granberg-Michaelson, *A Worldly Spirituality: The Call to Redeem Life on Earth* (San Francisco: Harper and Row, 1984).

Stanley Hauerwas, *A Community of Character: Toward a Constructive Christian Social Ethic* (Notre Dame, IN: University of Notre Dame Press, 1981).

Dieter Hessel, ed., *Social Themes of the Christian Year* (Geneva Press, 1983).

Urban T. Holmes, *The Priest in Community* (New York: Seabury, 1978).

Martin E. Marty, *The Word: People Participating in Preaching* (Philadelphia: Fortress, 1984).

Samuel D. Proctor, *Preaching About Crises in the Community* (Philadelphia: Westminster, 1987).

Ronald J. Sider and Darrel J. Brubaker, *Preaching on Peace* (Philadelphia: Fortress, 1982).

Ronald J. Sider and Michael A. King, *Preaching About Life in a Threatening World* (Philadelphia: Westminster, 1987).

Kelly Miller Smith, *Social Crisis Preaching* (Macon, GA: Mercer University Press, 1984).

William Stringfellow, *The Politics of Spirituality* (Philadelphia: Westminster, 1984).

William H. Willimon, *Preaching About Conflict in the Local Church* (Philadelphia: Westminster, 1987).

The Life-World of the Preacher

Walter Brueggemann, *The Prophetic Imagination* (Philadelphia: Fortress, 1987).

John Claypool, *The Light Within You* (Waco: Word, 1983).

_____, *The Preaching Event* (Waco: Word, 1980).

John S. Dunne, *A Search for God in Time and Memory* (Notre Dame, IN: University of Notre Dame Press, 1977).

Kathleen R. Fischer, *The Inner Rainbow: The Imagination in Christian Life* (New York: Paulist Press, 1983).

Kenneth L. Gibble, *The Preacher as Jacob: A New Paradigm for Preaching* (Minneapolis: Seabury, 1985).

Neil Q. Hamilton, *Maturing in the Christian Life: A Pastor's Guide* (Philadelphia: Westminster, 1984).

Urban T. Holmes, *Spirituality for Ministry* (New York: Harper and Row, 1982).

Reuben P. Job and Norman Shawchuck, *A Guide to Prayer for Ministers and Other Servants* (Nashville: The Upper Room, 1983).

Nelle Morton, *The Journey Is Home* (Boston: Beacon Press, 1985).

Henri, J. M. Nouwen, *The Wounded Healer* (New York: Doubleday, 1972).

_____, *Creative Ministry* (New York: Doubleday, 1978).

M. Scott Peck, *The Different Drum: Community Making and Peace* (New York: Simon and Schuster, 1987).

_____, *The Road Less Traveled* (New York: Simon and Schuster, 1983).

Thomas H. Troeger, *Creating Fresh Images for Preaching* (Valley Forge: Judson Press, 1982).

Hans van der Geest, trans. by Douglas W. Stott, *Presence in the Pulpit: The Impact of Personality in Preaching* (Atlanta: John Knox, 1981).

William H. Willimon, *Integrative Preaching: The Pulpit at the Center* (Nashville: Abingdon, 1981).

_____, *Worship as Pastoral Care* (Nashville: Abingdon, 1979).

Chapter 6
PROGRESS

How do I know whether or not I am making progress along this journey toward excellence in preaching? This is a very important question and a difficult one to answer. There is no absolute yardstick by which we can measure our growth in preaching. So much is dependent on the person of the preacher, the way that person views scripture, and the specific community of faith in which the preaching takes place.

We can look for guidelines, however, which will help us in assessing our work. In 1976 John Bergland published a brief essay entitled "Ten Tests for Preaching" which is very helpful in this respect. He notes at the conclusion of this essay that the criteria most frequently mentioned by laypersons are: "(1) Does the preacher offer anything of himself or herself?" (This usually is expressed, "Is the preacher sincere? Does the preacher really believe what is being said?") "Is this faithful to the scriptures?" (3) "Is it related to some real life need or concern?"[1]

In short, the laypersons in Bergland's article view wholeness in preaching as including the life-world of the preacher, the scripture, and the community. While the importance of these three worlds has been explored in previous chapters, this section offers ten specific suggestions for ways to assess preaching.

I will take the liberty to change the order of Bergland's ten tests, listing each under the life-world to which it most clearly relates.

The Life-World of the Scripture

The first question that the preacher needs to ask concerning the sermon's faithfulness to the life-world of the scriptures Bergland states this way: *"Is the sermon faithful to the biblical witness?"*[2] Have I taken a text out of its context? Have I imposed a meaning on the passage that is foreign to it? Have I looked at the passage in the larger context of the whole of the biblical witness? These are just a few of the questions that will help the preacher ascertain the sermon's faithfulness to the life-world of the scripture.

The second question Bergland raises related to this life-world is, *"Has the scripture passage been allowed to speak its own message?"*[3] Have I twisted the text to make it say what I wanted it to say? Have I toned down the more radical or demanding aspects of the text to make it more palatable? Have I really listened to the text for a word from God to me and this congregation? Again, these are significant questions for the preacher to ask of herself or himself.

The Life-World of the Community

In the life-world of the community, Bergland lists four issues that assist in evaluating our growth in preaching. The first of these is, *"Does the sermon address some ultimate and urgent need in life?"*[4] Is the congregation left asking "So what?" when the sermon is finished? Are the needs my preaching addresses both ultimate and urgent? Have I listened sufficiently to the life stories and experiences of my listeners to know what needs are ultimate and urgent for them?

The second question raised by Bergland is, *"Does the sermon encourage the spontaneous flight of mood and feeling?"*[5] Have I engaged the emotions and imaginations of the listeners as well as their intellects? Have I given them the freedom to take off in their own directions with the stories, images, and ideas of the sermon? Have I tried too hard to control the responses of my listeners and restricted their flights into memory of their past or dreams for the future?

Bergland's third test related to the community is stated this way, *"Does the sermon faithfully present both judgment and grace?"*[6] Have I given more bad news than good news in my sermons? Do I offer cheap grace and rationalize away the demands of the gospel? Have I experienced the judgment and grace of God in my own life sufficiently to share it as a testimony of faith?

Finally, Bergland asks, *"Is the sermon for all people?"*[7] Is my preaching inviting of all people to experience the judgment and grace of God and to respond? Are my examples and language inclusive of male and female; child, youth and adult; and persons of various languages, customs, and abilities as these are represented in the community of faith? Is my preaching motivated by a genuine care for the persons who listen?

The Life-World of the Preacher

There are four tests for preaching related to the life-world of the preacher in Bergland's view. First, he asks, *"Is the sermon thoughtful and informed?"*[8] Did I begin my work sufficiently early to study well and really give thought to my preaching? Did I look at a wide range of resources in preparing to preach? Do I read the newspapers, watch the television programs, and read the books and magazines that inform my listeners' lives and faith?

The second test for this life-world is, *"Does the preacher offer anything of himself or herself? Is the preacher present?"*[9] Does my preaching draw upon my own life experiences to find a common human connection with my listeners? When I preach, am I speaking with those present, or am I reading what was completed in the past and could just as well have been mailed out for them to read? Are my feelings toward my subject and those with whom I speak revealed in both the content and the attitude of my preaching?

Bergland states his third question, *"Is the preaching forthright, candid, and bold?"*[10] Am I being truly honest with the congregation in my preaching? Am I willing to speak a prophetic word when necessary, even though it calls my own life and the lives of my listeners to accountability? Am I more concerned with being liked or respected for my preaching than I am to speak the truth in whatever form, no matter how limited, it has been revealed to me?

The last test for preaching related to the life-world of the preacher asks, *"Is the preached word caring, responsive, and faithfully dialogical?*"[11] When I preach, are my words motivated by compassion for those who listen or to get back at them or put them down? Do I include myself in the words of both judgment and grace, refusing to see my role as above those who listen? Do I listen for and encourage honest feelings and ideas in response to my preaching and show a willingness to hear views different from my own?

These ten tests provide a valuable set of guidelines for us to assess our progress toward excellence in preaching. What we are about when we preach is important enough to take the time to do it well. This involves study of the Bible, involvement in the community, and a considerable self-knowledge. Make no mistake; our journey is not over. The quest for maturity in faith and excellence in preaching has just begun.

1. John Bergland, "Ten Tests for Preaching," *The Duke Divinity School Review* (Winter 1976), p. 20.
2. Ibid., p. 17.
3. Ibid., p. 18.
4. Ibid.
5. Ibid.
6. Ibid., p. 19.
7. Ibid., p. 20.
8. Ibid., p. 18.
9. Ibid., p. 19.
10. Ibid.
11. Ibid., p. 20.